The NAVAGRAHAS

Nine Celestial Bodies

This book belongs to:

____

Om KIDZ
An imprint of Om Books International

Adityaayacah Somaaya
Mangalaaya Budhaayacah
Guru Shukra Shanibyascha
Raahave Ketave Namah

ॐ आदित्याय च सोमाय मङ्गळाय बुधाय च।
गुरु शुक्र शनिभ्यश्च राहवे केतवे नमः॥

What are the Navagrahas?

The Navagrahas are celestial bodies that impact the lives of all beings on Earth. They include the Sun, the Moon, some planets and two lunar nodes or shadow planets. They gift each one of us unique qualities and make us special. Knowing a little bit about them helps us feel a closer connection to them and also appreciate these qualities in others.

Each of the Navagrahas is associated with a specific colour, gem, grain, animal, tree, day of the week, and zodiac sign. In this book, we will learn about this beautiful connection between the celestial bodies and us.

SURYA

SUN

Om Bhaskaraaya Vidmahe
Mahatdhyutikaraaya Dheemahi
Thanno Aditya Prachodayaat
ॐ भास्कराय विद्महे महद्युतिकराय धीमहि ।
तन्नो आदित्य प्रचोदयात् ।।

Simha (Leo)

Sun is the leader, the King, and he gives us leadership qualities. He rides a chariot of seven horses symbolising the seven colours in white light. The Sun rises and brings life. Flowers blossom, birds chirp and sing, and all activities begin. We pray to the Sun, who is the giver of life, to also fill our mind with the light of knowledge and truth. The Sun rules the rhythms in the Universe and blesses us with a sense of rhythm in music and dance.

CHANDRA
Pearl
Deer

MOON

Om Nishaakaraaya Vidmahe
Kalaanaathaya Dheemahi
Thannah Chandrah Prachodayaat

ॐ निशाकराय विद्महे कालनाथाय धीमहि।
तन्नः चन्द्रः प्रचोदयात्॥

Chandra is the moon and has a say over our minds. He gives us a pleasing and cool personality. When your mind is free from worries, full of joy, it shines with the beauty and coolness of the moon! A vivid imagination and poetic skills are gifts from Chandra.

MANGAL
Mesha (Aries)
Red Coral
Ram

Vrischika (Scorpio)

MARS

Om Angaarakaaya Vidmahe
Bhoomipaalaaya Dheemahi
Thannah Kujah Prachodayaat

ॐ अंगारकाय विद्महे भूमिपालाय धीमहि।
तन्नः कुजः प्रचोदयात्॥

Mars or Mangal is the warrior. Mars gives us broad shoulders, lots of courage, strength and patience. He loves gardening and agriculture. By spending time caring for Mother Earth, you can get the blessings of Mars.

Khadira

Red Lentil

BUDHA
Emerald
Yali

Kanya (Virgo)

Mithuna (Gemini)

MERCURY

Om Buddhgrahaaya Vidmahe
Induputraaya Dheemahi
Thannah Sowmyah Prachodayaat

ॐ बुद्धग्रहाय विद्महे इन्दुपुत्राय धीमहि।
तन्नः सौम्यः प्रचोदयात्॥

Mercury or Budha is the Prince. He is very intelligent and excellent at communication. He moves very swiftly and makes us intelligent, learned and wise.

Dhanuh (Sagittarius)
GURU
Yellow Sapphire
Chickpea

Meena (Pisces)

JUPITER

Om Suraachaaryaaya Vidmahe
Surashreshtaaya Dheemahi
Thanno Guruh Prachodayaat

ॐ सुराचार्याय विद्महे सुरश्रेष्ठाय धीमहि।
तन्नो गुरुः प्रचोदयात्।।

Jupiter is the Guru or Master. He is very compassionate and kind. He gives wisdom and also helps us to be good in studies. Guru is the biggest planet and gives us great protection.

Fig Tree
SHUKRA
Tula (Libra)
Diamond
Horse
White Beans

Vrushaba (Taurus)

VENUS

Om Rajathaabhaaya Vidmahe
Bhrigusutaaya Dheemahi
Thanno Shukrah Prachodayaat

ॐ रजदाभाय विद्महे भृगुसुताय धीमहि।
तन्नो शुक्रः प्रचोदयात्॥

Shukra is a great artist! He is associated with the planet Venus. He helps us to be creative and appreciate beauty in everything. He makes us friendly, charming and popular among friends.

SHANI
Saturn
Blue Sapphire
Shami Tree
Crow
Lord Shiva
Black Sesame Laddoo

Kumbh (Aquarius)

SATURN

Om Sanaischaraaya Vidhmahe
Chaayaaputraaya Dheemahi
Thanno Mandah Prachodayaat

ॐ शनैश्चराय विद्महे छायापुत्राय धीमहि।
तन्नो मन्दः प्रचोदयात्॥

Shani Dev is the god who makes you sincere and hardworking. He loves discipline. He is an ardent devotee of Lord Shiva. He helps everybody slow down and relax, and encourages one to share. His favourite colour is black and midnight blue just like the night with a million twinkling stars!

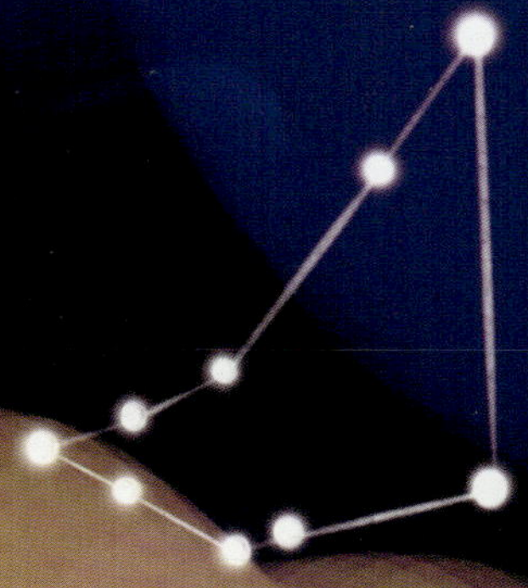

Makara (Capricorn)

RAHU
Hessonite
Lion

ASCENDING NODE

Om Shukadantaaya Vidmahe
Ugrarupaaya Dheemahi
Thanno Raahuh Prachodayaat

ॐ शुकदन्ताय विद्महे उग्ररूपाय धीमहि।
तन्नो राहुः प्रचोदयात्॥

Rahu is the soldier. Rahu makes you very innovative. There are no zodiac signs associated with Rahu. His favourite colour is red and black and his vahana is the lion. His plant is the durva grass and his grain is the black gram. His favourite jewel is Hessonite.

KETU
Kusha Grass
Cat's Eye
Fish

DESCENDING NODE

Om Chitravarnaaya Vidmahe
Sarparupaaya Dheemahi
Thannah Kethuh Prachodayaat

ॐ चित्रवर्णाय विद्महे सर्परूपाय धीमहि।
तन्नः केतुः प्रचोदयात्॥

Ketu is a soldier. Ketu helps you enquire about the purpose of life and have a higher goal. There are no zodiac signs associated with Ketu. His favourite colour is grey and he also loves anything that is multi-coloured. His vahana is the fish. His plant is the Kusha grass and his grain is the horse gram. Ketu's favourite gemstone is the cat's eye. Ketu brings you freedom.

Horse Gram

When we meditate, do yoga and pranayama and chant
"Om Namah Shivaya", we get the blessings of all the Navagrahas.

SURYA

Colour - Maroon

Grain - Wheat

Vahana- Horse Chariot

Gem - Ruby

Plant - White Arka

Day - Sunday

Zodiac - Simha (Leo)

CHANDRA

Colour - White

Grain - Rice

Vahana - Deer

Gem - Pearl

Tree - Palasha (flame of the forest)

Day - Monday

Zodiac - Kataka (Cancer)

MANGAL

Colour - Red

Grain - Red Lentil

Vahana - Ram

Gem - Red Coral

Tree - Khadira

Day - Tuesday

Zodiac - Vrischika (Scorpio) &
Mesha (Aries)

BUDHA

Colour - Green

Grain - Green Gram

Vahana- Mystical Yali

Gem - Emerald

Plant - Apamarga

Day - Wednesday

Zodiac - Kanya (Virgo) &
Mithuna (Gemini)

GURU

Colour - Yellow

Grain - Chickpea

Vahana- Elephant

Gem - Yellow Sapphire

Tree - Peepal

Day - Thursday

Zodiac - Dhanush (Sagittarius) &
Meena (Pisces)

SHUKRA

Colour - White

Grain - White Beans

Vahana - Horse

Gem - Diamond

Plant - Fig Tree

Day - Friday

Zodiac - Vrushaba (Taurus) &
Tula (Libra)

SHANI

Colour - Midnight Blue

Grain - Black Sesame

Vahana - Crow

Gem - Blue Sapphire

Tree - Shami Tree

Day - Saturday

Zodiac - Makara (Capricorn) &
Kumbha (Aquarius)

RAHU

Colour - Black

Grain - Black Gram

Vahana - Lion

Gem - Hessonite

Plant - Durva Grass

Day - None

Zodiac - None

KETU

Colour - Grey and Multicolour

Grain - Horse Gram

Vahana - Fish

Gem - Cat's Eye

Plant - Kusha Grass

Day - None

Zodiac - None